THE POISON OF WHITE SUPREMACY.

Why The Killings In Buffalo Is Plain Stupidity.

By

Theophilus David.

Introduction.

If you care about humanity, if you believe that we are all important in the sight of the One who made us, if it's also a burning desire in our heart as it is online that one day there will be perfect peace in this world, then keep on reading as I take you on the journey to the beginnings of White supremacy and what you and I can do to tackle it and overcome it.

Now, let's ride, I assure you it will be mind shifting and will radically awaken that fire within your bosom to ensure there's peace on Earth.

Chapter 1.

White Supremacy:
Definition, History, Examples, and Facts.

Supremacy of Whites:

White supremacy is a word used to describe a set of beliefs in which one or more of the following basic concepts are central:

1) Whites should have domination over members of other races, especially when they may co-exist.

2) Whites should live alone in a whites-only society.

3) White people have a superior "culture" to other civilizations.

4) White people are genetically superior to others. White supremacy, as a full-fledged ideology, encompasses far more than simple racism or bigotry.

Most white supremacists now think that the white race is in danger of extinction as a result of a growing "flood" of non-whites who are controlled and influenced by Jews and that immediate action is required to "rescue" the white race.

White supremacy refers to views and generalities that the lighter-barked/, skinned, or" white," mortal races are naturally superior to other ethnical groups.

The word "white racist" is now used to characterize colorful groups that cleave to an ultranationalist, supremacist, or fascist testaments. White supremacist organizations have constantly used violence to attain their objects.

According to to19th-century British pens similar to Rudyard Kipling, Charles Kingsley, Thomas Carlyle, and others, it was the duty of Europeans — the "white man's burden" — to bring civilization to nonwhite peoples through beneficent imperialism. Several attempts were made to give white supremacy a scientific footing, as colorful institutes and famed scientists published findings asserting the natural superiority of whites. Those ideas were bolstered in the early 20th century by the new wisdom of intelligence testing, which purported to show major differences in intelligence between the races. In similar tests, northern Europeans always scored more advanced than Africans.

From the nineteenth through the mid-twentieth century, political leaders and social scientists in Europe and the United States took white supremacy for granted.

For illustration, the French pen and diplomatist Arthur de Gobineau wrote about the superiority of the white race in his four-volume Essai surl'inégalité des races humaines (1853 – 55; Essay on the Inequality of Mortal Races), claiming that Aryans (Germanic peoples) represented the loftiest position of mortal development. It was the "white man's burden," according to 19th-century British intellectualists similar to Rudyard Kipling, Charles Kingsley, Thomas Carlyle, and others, for Europeans to deliver civilization to nonwhite peoples through benign imperialism. Colorful institutes and notable scientists have tried to give white supremacy a scientific foundation.

Several attempts were made to give white supremacy a scientific foundation, with conclusions claiming whites' natural superiority published by colorful institutes and notable scientists. The arising wisdom of IQ testing, which claimed to show large differences in intelligence between races, strengthened those sundries in the early twentieth century. Northern Europeans constantly outperformed Africans in analogous tests.

White supremacy gained wide political support in the United States during the age of slavery and the preceding Jim Crow period of legal ethnical isolation, just as it did in contemporary European social governments. Although numerous peaceful individualities and organizations believed forcefully in white supremacist views, the news was especially linked with violent groups similar to the Ku Klux Klan (KKK), which has endured some success in the United States of America (particularly in the 1920s). Overtly racist testaments, on the other hand, had fallen out of favor across important of the Western world by the mid-1950s, a development whisked by both racism and decolonization.

White supremacy was revived in the United States in the late 1950s and early 1960s as a result of hostility among some American whites toward the American civil rights movement, and civil rights legislation, particularly the Civil Rights Act (1964) and the Voting Rights Act (1965), and Supreme Court opinions vacating numerous racially discriminative laws, particularly Brown. Board of Education of Topeka (1954). It eventually showed itself in the "White Power" movement, which formed in response to the 1960s and 1970s "Black Power" beliefs. The United States government's countersign of or participation in measures similar as affirmative action, academy busing, and proscriptions against ethnical demarcation in the casing request scarified white racialists and numerous social rightists. Their dissatisfaction.

Their resentment fueled the rise of different white racist associations and movements, including the classic KKK, colorful neo-Nazi associations, and religious Christian Identity groups. Indeed, by the alternate half of the twentieth century, the Christian Identity movement — which claimed that northern Europeans were descended directly from biblical lines of Israel and that the impending Armageddon would affect a final battle of whites against nonwhites — had come the dominant religious standpoint of white racialists in the United States.

White racialists in the United States and around the world, still, were ultimately unfit to uphold laws that guaranteed white dominance. Rhodesia, which changed its name to Zimbabwe after ceding control to its white nonage in 1980, and South Africa, whose intolerance system was destroyed in the 1990s, were the last administrations to institutionalize white supremacy doctrines through complete legislation.

White supremacy has thrived as a populist gospel despite the repeal of racialist and discriminative laws across the Western world and in Africa. During the 1970s and 1980s, white racialists' decreasingly harmonious converse and imagery gained dominance in Europe, where immigration, particularly from former colonies in Asia, Africa, and the Caribbean, contributed to a considerable and growing nonwhite population. In some countries, anti-immigrant political parties similar as the

National Front (Front National) in France, the Republicans (Die Republikaner) in Germany, the Freedom Party of Austria (Freiheitliche Partei sterreichs), and (since 2005) the Alliance for the Future of Austria (Bündnis Zukunft sterreich) have expressed white racist ideas in their platforms. Following the election the former time, in 2009.

Following the election of Barack Obama, the first African-American chairman of the United States, in 2008, the US Department of Homeland Security and the Federal Bureau of Investigation (FBI) advised that white racist groups and right-sect regulars were retaining new members by supersizing fears of gun control and expanded weal rolls, as well as exploiting resentment created by the profitable recession that began in late 2007. Still, some spectators of the movements questioned their allegations.

White supremacists and so-called white nationalists largely disavowed racism but celebrated "white" identity and lamented the alleged erosion of white political and economic power and the decline of white culture during Donald J. Trump's presidential campaign in early 2016, which gained strong support from white supremacists and so-called white nationalists, in the face of non-white immigration and multiculturalism Trump's followers included members of the "alt-right" (alternative right) movement, a loose collection of relatively young white supremacists, white nationalists, radical libertarians, and neo-Nazis. Trump has previously cast doubt on Obama's American birth certificate and made racist comments on immigrants and ethnic minorities during his campaign, promising to erect a wall along the US-Mexico border and deport some 11 million people residing in the country, especially the Mexicans and the Muslims.

It's entrenched deeply in the American Society, the absurdity and foolishness that we as whites are better than the blacks, nothing could be farther from the truth.

Now, in the next chapter, let me give you four reasons or ways White Supremacy Harms Humanity.

Chapter 2.

4 Ways White Supremacy Harms Humanity.

It is critical to respect the words of Angela Davis, a scholar, and activist. "The need for public talks on race and racism is also a plea to build a vocabulary that helps us to have informed conversations," Davis said in her book Freedom is a Constant Struggle.

Our awareness of racism would remain shallow if we try to employ historically outmoded languages." For the sake of this book, the term white supremacy will be used throughout because it is the most widely recognized.

However, some have argued that we should avoid using the word "white supremacy" since it suggests that those who are racialized as white are "superior" to others.

It should be noted, however, that some have urged us to avoid using the phrase "white supremacy" because it suggests that those who are racialized as white are "superior" to persons of other races. The concepts of white perversion and white insecurity have been proposed as replacements for the term white supremacy.

Here are the four ways White Supremacy harms humanity.

1. It stifles creativity.

One of the ways white supremacy damages mankind is by preventing us from using our imaginations. "When it comes to black life in America, there's only one conclusion I can reach about some white people: You don't care to put yourself in our shoes," American film director Kasi Lemmons said in an op-ed for The Washington Post. For black Americans, the implications of this lack of imagination are fatal."

This lack of imagination inhibits creativity and fosters the appropriation of other people's ideas. This is not a new occurrence, and it goes beyond intellectual property. The enslavement and bloodshed against Indigenous peoples perpetrated by Christopher Columbus are classic examples of white supremacist behavior. Women of color.

For example, black women have ignited several global social movements, but they are frequently left out of these movements or aren't given the recognition they deserve. White supremacy can lead to the adoption of learned helplessness in marginalized and oppressed cultures. Learned helplessness describes how a person feels when they have little to no control over a circumstance. They feel powerless, and they don't seek out opportunities to improve or influence their circumstances because they believe they can't.

Because white supremacy has driven them to believe that there is nothing they can do, a young Black child living in an under-resourced and impoverished community may develop an attitude of learned helplessness.

White supremacy limits our ability to think, create, and conceive a world that is different from our own, as well as our ability to come up with new and original ideas.

2. It is self-centered.
"Whiteness always attempts to center itself," said Joquina Reed, a DEI consultant, and anti-racism instructor. Individualism and independence are reinforced by white supremacy culture, which draws us away from our origins in a community-oriented attitude. Those who are most damaged and oppressed by the systems and structures in which we live will be more harmed and oppressed in a society where we prioritize ourselves over others.

We witnessed this with the Covid-19 endemic—there have been objections from elements of the populace who believe mask regulations infringe on their "individual rights" in several nations. It doesn't matter if research shows that many of these advised health precautions will help prevent the spread of a fatal virus—no one seems to care.

There is little respect for how our activities affect our community, regardless of whether science indicates that many of these suggested health precautions can reduce the spread of a lethal epidemic. From the American Civil Rights Movement to Malala Yousafzai's story, some of the most powerful instances of social change have occurred when the needs of others are emphasized and pushed for.

It takes a village to raise a single child, just as the African proverb goes. We are all interconnected and formed by the individuals in our immediate neighborhoods. Humans are sociable beings that can't survive or thrive in isolation. White supremacy aims to erode our sense of community and divert our attention away from other people's concerns and needs.

Self-centeredness and arrogance destroy any society's fabric. Individual needs, wants, and desires have taken humanity away from its fundamental core.

3. It promotes perfectionism.
Monique Melton, an anti-racism educator, frequently speaks about the risks of our obsession with perfection

and teaches seminars on how to break the perfectionism loop. **"Perfectionism is white supremacy by another name,"** Melton has said. Perfectionism won't keep you safe, and it won't help you heal." Everyone is harmed by society's fixation with perfection. Women, for example, are held to be the pinnacles of perfection in our culture, balancing parenthood and full-time work with ease. We saw this in the stories about poisonous female bosses and the glorification of the ambitious woman who "had it all" while juggling parenting and work.

Women who are deemed successful in society are frequently asked how they manage to "do it all"—a question that is frequently asked.

Successful women are frequently asked how they manage to "do it all," a question that is rarely, if ever, asked of men. In the office, our preoccupation with perfection is also damaging. Tema Okun compiled a list of white supremacist characteristics that manifest themselves in organizations; perfectionism was one of the traits that manifested itself in a variety of ways. Perfectionism fails to recognize and appreciate how an employee achieves great achievements, instead of focusing on the person's failures.

According to Okun, this adds to low employee morale by creating an environment where employees are more likely to express criticism.

~ A perfectionism-promoting culture is one in which people are denied the opportunity to express themselves.

~ A perfectionism-promoting society is one in which people are denied the room or opportunity to grow, instead of focusing on "fixing" what is wrong rather than realizing that mistakes are an essential part of the process.

4. Mindset of scarcity.
We are encouraged to believe that we must compete with others by white supremacy. It advocates the idea that the only way to rise is to be better, wiser, and stronger than others. White supremacy does not promote collaboration or admit that everyone who has achieved a semblance of what society considers "success" has done so with the assistance of others—success is not a solo sport. The rivalry mindset that capitalism instills in us leads us to believe that we are competing for a finite amount of resources. The world is rich and abundant. We must acknowledge that there is enough room for all of us to produce products and services without feeling confined.

Yes, we must acknowledge that there is enough room for all of us to create products and services without feeling as if just one of us can do so. We must recognize that we are not in competition with one another, as white supremacy would have us believe. Adopting a scarcity mindset encourages us to feel that we must make the most money possible by using the cheapest means possible, thus abusing the work of others, which is frequently the labor of society's most disadvantaged and oppressed. By rejecting the scarcity perspective and adopting an abundance attitude, we will be able to achieve great things that will benefit society as a whole.

Chapter 3.
Solid Lessons From The Buffalo Shooting.

On the autumn of 14 May 2022, a heavily fortified youthful man in military gear attacked shoppers and workers at a supermarket in Buffalo, New York, killing ten people and wounding three others. Utmost of the victims were Black – the supermarket is located in a generally Black neighborhood – with the shooter specifically targeting Black individualities, and reported as abstaining from attacking white individualities.

The firing was live-streamed via the gaming platform Twitch, recorded using a helmet camera, and echoing the aesthetics of popular first-person shooter games. In the moments previous to the firing, the perpetrator released an online fiat – a tactic seen in several other recent extreme right blowups. In it, he specifically spoke of targeting Black non ages in the US, blending ethnical conspiracy propositions of 'white relief with rabid antisemitism and anti-transgender statements in an enmeshing of online conspiracies and far-right memes.

Public officers, similar to New York Governor Kathy Hochul classified the firing as white supremacy terrorism, calling on social media platforms to up their game in covering online hate speech, " especially when it's directed against (nonage) populations and comes under the guise of white supremacy terrorism, which is exactly what happens then in Buffalo".

Still, there's concern that the spread of violent rights-sect statements online and high-profile cases of white racism and incel violence aren't being taken seriously nor adequately dealt with by authorities.

With Western governments facing review on either their poor record of responding to the extreme right or, in some cases, their active incuriosity towards the spread of extreme-right narratives in the corridor of mainstream society, it's important to consider what acceptable responses to the extreme right online could look like. This should include responses to the measurable increase in online hate speech, doxing and importunity, extreme right propaganda rotation, and the mainstreaming of rudiments of far-right testaments – along with preceding occurrences of violence.

May 15th marked the anniversary of the Christchurch Call, an transnational political commitment by governments and tech companies to exclude terrorist and violent revolutionist content online – a call established and named after the butchery of 51 Muslims at the hands of a far-right bushwhacker, which reinforces the significance and urgency of this issue.

Drawing on the Buffalo firing, this perspective considers what perceptivity can be gathered to potentially attack violent right- sect content online and its impacts in Europe, the US, and beyond.

This perspective offers an examination of the fiat through the lens of being responses to far-right unreasonableness, examining the Buffalo case to offer recommendations on how Western governments and mainstream social media companies could respond to violence linked to engagement with revolutionist accouterments participated and circulated online.

It is found that extreme-right attacks aim to capture public attention, frequently as the primary means for propagating extreme-right ideas into the mainstream. The fiat is, in part, a living document, part of a process of streamlining and passing on extreme-right narratives from one bushwhacker to another. As well as reflecting current extreme-right dialogues, it also evidences the transference of ideas from the political mainstream towards the extreme-right, with the mainstream converse shaping the central corridor of the fiat.

Current governmental and private sector responses struggle to adequately deal with similar documents due to a combination of factors over-reliance on takedowns, difficulties in collaboration between governments and social media platforms – but also because current approaches exceptionalism the nature of extreme-right violence as dissociated from mainstream converse. Challenging this conceptualization may offer a path to a more effective, lower security-centric response against extreme-right violence.

Extreme right violent content online – issues raised by the Buffalo shooter

(You have to be careful of what you read online, you can't say you'll tackle white supremacy or any "hate" movement sponsored from Hell and be consuming negative content if you're doing so, please, stop it).

There are several counter-accusations for how government actors presently interact with and can respond to far-right violence, which we can ripen from the firing and the fiat. These concentrate largely on the challenges of dealing with the accouterments themselves, as well as responding to the types of content they contain.
The rotation and impacts of manifestos online

Originally, the nature of the firing demonstrates that the killer drew heavily on inventions and practices of former attacks, and contemporaneously also aimed to extensively circulate a fiat. There's significant substantiation of memetic reduplication in the fiat, of reliance on textbooks, maps, and images planted extensively amongst right-sect online communities. The fiat also contains ideas, including in-and out- group architectures, that have been reproduced from former manifestos, passed from one bushwhacker to the coming. This includes specific conceptualizations similar to the Great Relief proposition apparent in textbooks and statements from Anders Breivik, Dylann Roof, and Patrick Wood Crusius, as well as a significant quantum of textbooks and filmland that have been dupe-pasted directly from the document of the Christchurch bushwhacker Brenton Tarrant.

Similarly, it makes sense to consider manifestos as a type of palimpsest, a form of living document, that details white racist testaments and their means of articulating these in violent action.
While manifestos are frequently framed as a product of the firing, it may be more accurate to suggest that the attack operates as a political means of encouraging and enabling a wider readership of the fiat. The public nature of the firing and the posterior ineluctable scramble of media to read and broadcast its core tenets are crucial processes in the whitewashing of violence, leading to the spreading of core fascist ideas, conspiracy propositions of white relief, and the practical means for others in carrying out unborn attacks.

Therefore, violence is just one strategy to encourage a more core end of enabling a wider readership of far-right ideas. When we consider how to fight similar documents and the dialogues they embody, thus, it may be prudent to suppose beyond takedowns, as they feel to be ineffective against such a living document that's circulated ahead and during an attack, is fluently reproduced, and is indeed participated as a whole or in part by media organizations or judges.

As we link evil content online to violence offline, it's important to note that in a functional position, law enforcement faces significant challenges in diving into this type of content particularly as there isn't always a clear link between online behaviors and offline violence.

Indeed, in the face of an attack, police are frequently criticized for not having acted on former "suspicious online geste" – the suspect, in this case, had preliminarily been flagged for making pitfalls and had spent time in sanitarium evaluations.

Still, law enforcement is frequently under-equipped or under-staffed for the kind of webbing that such a "pre-crime" approach would number, not to mention the substantial breaches in civil rights and liberties it would potentially number. Also, while online hate speech can incite real-world violence, there's inadequate substantiation that connects an advanced rate of online exertion, on an individual position, with an advanced likeliness of committing real-life violence.

Therefore, an overreliance by law enforcement and security actors on online geste as a predictor of the violence couldn't yield the asked goods.

To complicate matters further, significant quantities of extreme right content online aren't visibly racist or can incontinently be flagged as incitement to violence. Some of the most insidious promoters of hate speech are far-right influencers tone- placarded libertarian and conservative online actors who play a crucial part in promoting supremacist and white nationalist views in mainstream online spaces.

A study of the use of dar-right symbols across transnational surrounds has shown that, in online spaces, far-right actors have tended to avoid the use of further egregious imagery and ensigns linked to public illiberalism, rather preferring to use' cryptic imagery, where the far-right messaging is hidden or largely environment-dependent. Current approaches to online content responses by governments and supra-governmental bodies have tended to prioritize proscription lists and the identification of interdicted organizational ensigns, floundering to deal with this further cryptic far-right content. The use of further mainstreamed imagery in the fiat document, therefore, hints toward the need for lesser work relating to far-right language and images within the environment.

The feat demonstrates how the bushwhacker frames himself in the wider far-right scene. White racist blowups feel to operate decreasingly singly from the confines of formal far-right groups, and the perpetrator of the Buffalo firing made it clear that he neither supports, nor is he operating as a part of a group, yet still considers himself as a fascist and a terrorist, that's terrible.

The document and the nature of the firing accentuate this lack of group involvement, with unequivocal statements by the bushwhacker stating that they were radicalized online and had little offline relations with those of analogous views. These statements corroborate being exploration suggesting that far-right climates are largely atomized, linked internationally through international online engagement rather than part of the class to the decreasingly less new-fascist groups.

The dependence on governmental responses to the far-right that calculate the identification of group ensigns or prescription lists, thus, is largely problematic in such an environment.

Importantly, measures to fairly invest governments with the authority to demand the erasure of online content are met with resistance by the public, including social activists and scholars. The extreme right has capitalized considerably on the extension of government authority and the abridging of individual liberties during the COVID-19 epidemic.

Similar measures have been routinely reframed as instruments of social control, government corruption, and state bastardy. The extension of government authority to internet providers and social media platforms is likely to be used also. Recent attempts have been made to address the far-right in Europe for case, in the governmental proscription of far-right groups, the construction of an EU-wide description of Violent Right-Wing Unreasonableness and work with major online platforms to challenge violent far-right content.

Still, current European policy is critiqued as containing a heavy Islamist bias', alongside a methodical underplaying and underestimation of neo-Nazism, white supremacism, and analogous homegrown far-right movements.

Practical guidance for conducting attacks

Vast tracts of textbooks within the document include the means for carrying an applicable magazine for the firing, the means for carrying out surveillance, the costs and effectiveness of different kinds of artillery and armor, and indeed cerebral conversations on how to make up confidence for the attack – all of which are strictly outlined. The document isn't just about testament and the spreading of far-right ideas, but their practical operation; the attack rested on occasion and means, just as important as testament. Consideration of how to address far-right violence that fails to deal with, or wholly obscures discussion on the means of addressing the available openings for similar violence and focuses rather only on testament, will thus insure an impoverished response.

Exercising mainstream narratives

One way of addressing the occasion environment for similar attacks is to consider the mainstream. White supremacism is shown – at least in this fiat – as responsive to mainstream conversations taking place online, interacting with and drawing upon public and transnational political debates.

The document deals heavily with antiquated conceptions, debunked racialism, and a set of propositions that are deeply embedded in fascist testaments and language with roots going numerous generations back. But they interweave traditional fascist language against artistic and political nonage communities with current events, constructing narratives that include conversations on cryptocurrency, transgender rights, environmental enterprises, pornography, transnational affairs, and prominent contemporary nonage politicians.

Similarly, to respond to the trouble posed by the extreme right, there must be work conducted not just on understanding far-right testaments, but on how mainstream language influences far-right dialogues. Counter Accusations for the private sector responding to revolutionist content online.

Current governmental approaches to the far-right pause far behind attacks – there's substantiation that governments in the West aren't taking the trouble from the far-right seriously and may indeed be looking to roll back responses to similar unreasonableness. The uninterrupted replication of tactics online and offline in far-right bushwhackers also suggest that any approaches that are presently being enforced haven't yet had enough applicable impact to be effective. Given this geography of blurred lines and unclear boundaries between terrorist content junking and civil liberties, policy actors would profit from diversifying their approaches to online unreasonableness.

Both governmental and transnational organizations should start moving online forestallment sweats in a new direction that doesn't infringe so explosively on individual rights and with a lower eventuality to boomerang.

For illustration, governments could invest further in online knowledge education in seminaries to minimize the vulnerability of youthful people to online propaganda. Recognition of the part that anti-migrant,anti-minority and anti-transgender language in public media and politics has in similar attacks may also have counter-accusations for effective response against far-right violence. As this firing and fiat demonstrate, governmental approaches towards the far-right should be just as important and embedded in helping to appreciatively shape the mainstream debate as extreme testaments.

Crucial to the Christchurch Call is the need to address the live streaming of similar attacks. With the tactics still being stationed there, the further focus must be placed on practical means of precluding this.

The selection of Twitch by the Buffalo bushwhacker as the platform for Livestream, detailed in the fiat as the favored platform, has profound counter-accusations. Experimenters have been advising of the gamification of violence as "the use of game design rudiments in within-game surrounds".

Whilst it's important to caution against drawing a direct reason from videogame operation to offline violence, the adding applicability of game-like rudiments in revolutionist violence signals an artistic shift in the way violent actors frame their attacks and also distribute them.

Beyond its Internet aesthetic appeal, the gamification of real-life violence has other purposes. Originally, by reducing real-life mortal casualties to statistics victims come depersonalized.

Secondly, rephrasing casualties into score setting helps solidify the common ideal necessary to bind angry, youthful, English-speaking white men actors encyclopedia ally, from Christchurch to Pittsburgh, who feel ever insulated from their original community.

The Buffalo firing live-streaming echoes the tactics of the perpetrators of the Christchurch and Hanau blowups, who likewise participated in their atrocities live online and left behind manifestos to "explain" their conduct.

The purpose behind similar tactics is to serve as pieces of propaganda on the revolutionist online spheres

(4chan, 8chan, Discord, and certain areas of Reddit), as well as to shock and maneuver mainstream media outlets into engaging with their acts of violence.

For a terrorist, be it a tone-radicalized individual or a systematized group, any hype is good hype. Especially when this type of recording is likely to circulate on the internet for a long time – in some cases, for months after the platforms themselves have pledged to retire the content.

The actuality of these recordings and manifestos leads us to another thorny issue how are tech companies and hosting service providers meant to deal with right sect revolutionist content online? Whilst it can be delicate to determine revolutionist online content, there are also issues in drawing a line between admissible freedom of speech and extreme propaganda. Recent attempts to codify extreme right symbols by the European Commission and the Member States – a measure developed to support tech companies and groupings similar to the Global Internet Forum to Counter Terrorism (GIFCT) – have led to a limited agreement. Meanwhile, the development of the European standard description of Violent Right-Wing Unreasonableness has demanded a firm legal base – enforced only as a premonitory description and meeting with resistance or incuriosity from some EU Member States.

All legal and government enterprises regarding terrorist content online rest heavily on a public-private cooperation strategy. From the European Union's Regulation on the dispersion of terrorist content online to the fore-named Christchurch Call agreement, the main part is assigned to mainstream social media platforms similar to Twitter, YouTube, or Meta.

In a purely functional position, it's unclear whether tech companies' commitment to content temperance is backed up by the necessary help and specialized (algorithmic) coffers. Likewise, these enterprises ignore the important part of lower or further niche online spots in propaganda prolixity, as we've seen constantly with spots similar as Twitch, 4chan, or Discord. Eventually, governments are moreover floundering to or designedly avoiding, enforcing a legal description of Violent Right-Wing unreasonableness, and private tech companies, in turn, either don't have the legal capacity to understand colorful differing public approaches to what's legal or illegal in the environment of extreme-right speech or frame themselves as having a' popular deficiency about governments.

Private companies, thus, prefer to stick to the letter of the law – rather than the broader spirit of the law – in laundering content, suggesting it should eventually be over to tagged officers to determine the boundary at which controversial speech becomes hate speech or unreasonableness.

Conclusion

It's important to emphasize that extreme-right attacks aim to capture public attention, and manifestos and recordings of the butcheries are an as important a part of the attack as the killings themselves, as they contribute to further whitewashing of violence, expose the general public to spiteful borderline ideas, and generally give glorification to the actors whose deeds are subject of transnational commentary.

The junking of online content might feel like the logical conclusion to this problem. There are, still problems with this. Originally, simply removing terrorist content is delicate. There are deep political divides around the description (s) of the extreme right, as well as important specialized dissensions. The part of private actors, whilst important talked upon, has so far been only mildly encouraging, and much further commitment on the part of big tech companies may be demanded to move forward.

Secondly, junking of manifestos isn't enough to ensure the protection of the general population against hate speech and hate crimes. The online sphere is a dynamic, digressive terrain, and living textbooks and terrorist manifestos embody similar malleability, with their admixture of memes, intimation, and conspiracy propositions. Indeed in the event of successful and total junking, similar content – from images to infographics, to propositions – was drawn from online spheres in the first place. Therefore, removing manifestos would not be enough, as they would simply be drawn up again by new actors. One result could be removing an inconceivable quantum of content from the internet, but the feasibility of similar measures is questionable.

Still, the disincentivizing of similar attacks does present a possible avenue for further disquisition by government and private bodies. Therefore, we endorse the development of indispensable policy directions which try not to suppress, but to offset, extreme right content online. This can include the use of digital knowledge tools for adding citizen adaptability to propaganda and the dispersion of hate online and offline. This must mean the development of practices erected upon examination of both the testament and the occasion environment that were handed to former bushwhackers, as well as critical discussion on the part of the mainstream in extreme-right attacks, developing a practice that's cognizant of the part that mainstream debate in enabling the radicalization of beliefs online.

Finally, it's important as a Christian nation founded on the authority and authenticity of God's Word that we all realize that all these hate speeches, and hate movements of which White Supremacy is part are all inspired by the Devil, the father of all lies, deceits, and hatred.

Until we all come to realize what the One who declared on the cross that It Is Finished has done for us, we will keep hating each other, the fact is that we are of one blood created by the same God who loves us all equally and so let's bow in humble adoration of who He is and how magnificently made every human is and as we keep our eyes focused on Jesus, the Son of God, we will be full of His love and extend it to everyone as well.

God bless you!
God bless the United States of America.